The Station Before

The Station Before

Linda Anderson

First published 2020 by
Liverpool University Press
4 Cambridge Street
Liverpool
L69 7ZU

British Library Cataloguing-in-Publication data
A British Library CIP record is available

ISBN 978-1-789-62167-9 softback

Typeset by Carnegie Book Production, Lancaster
Printed and bound in Poland by Booksfactory.co.uk

In poetry the number of beginnings so far exceeds the number of endings that we cannot even conceive of it.

Mary Ruefle, *Madness, Rack and Honey*

If you are lucky, you may experience a moment *before.*

Susan Howe, *Spontaneous Particulars:*
The Telepathy of Archives

The Photographer and the Balloon

I'd prepared it all for days
the balloon, my laboratory
in the basket underneath,
the lens opening its heavy eye,
the yellow aphotogenic glass.

I thought I'd capture it:
the way I drifted between
nuances and combinations as if
they were the same, everything
in focus, formal, inexhaustible.

Nothing and yet again nothing.
A series all in black, without even
a shadow, the fuliginous
plates were smothered, drowned.
I gave up hope and slept.

Next day the balloon had folded
in on itself like a flower head
in the rain, perched on its pedicel.
I divested myself of all I could –
my boots, my coat, my necktie –

and rose a little way into the air.
The day was overcast. Cold.
Thick drizzle sleeked the lens.
But this time when I looked
I could see an image bit by bit appear

pale, masked by a hazy atmosphere,
stained by all the attempts there'd
been before. But what does seeing mean?
I was looking through a door, half-open,
at two white doves just landed there.

Kindred

The varnished grain of wood on the door.
Heavy to open; swings shut easily.

His desk with the Bible.
The glass book shelves behind him.

She knows not to interrupt.
She has let him down.

She would not understand in any case.
She gives what she can.

He will write her epitaph one day.
She tried but was a slow learner.

       *

Shepherd of souls
The sheep on the braes of Meikle.

The ploughed fields, seagulls pecking
at the earth.

She in bare feet, 12 years old.
Sun twinkling on the water.

The pilgrim flock
Gathered in, the gate closing

behind them, behind
her memories.

       *

The voices on the wires
he's buried deep underground

in Arras, in Albert, in Cambrai.
The receiver is faraway.

Once he slept in a deserted
German trench.

She imagines him wandering
across rutted fields. A stranger.

When the guns cease,
there's nothing but silence in the air.

       *

An April fool, that was
what she was,

searching his desk
for something not there.

She dreams of a farmhouse
they could rent in summer

with eggs for the collecting,
wood for the chopping.

He sits silently. Takes himself
silently off to bed, *as usual.*

       *

The river flowing inwards.
She thinks of the darkness

a torrent of silence
bearing down

The shadow of the wings
The everlasting arms.

Yet windswept moments
lightly catch at her

the ordinary sensation she
holds, untransfigured

Crossing

Imagine arriving from one of the four corners
for the world was already wide then,

sundered, slumped in the ship's stern,
ear to the swell of nothingness,

feet bound in fraying rags, half-starved,
history flying ahead, unfastened,

and the lurch to landfall. *Where am I?*
Fealty, faith, a congregation

of kittiwakes. Your plain heart's song.
Snow and rain mingle on the cliff-tops

where God's presence is in the keening of wind
across the whin-sill, thorns of gorse.

A life measured in winters. This small plot,
a parable of growing and sorrow

and fate. The end of the world.
Still tender within the tracks to another.

Lion

To know the language and have time to be in it and to move slowly

Ernest Hemingway, *Green Hills of Africa*

Afterwards I looked for the mountains on a map,
wondered if the blueness we saw through layers

of mist was these, the Kipengere range known also
as the Livingstone mountains, or closer up, Kipa.

At night came rain. Great gusts launching against
the canvas; in the darkness lightning flashes,

our white faces. Bones strewn across the sandy flats,
river-crossings swollen by rain, the bottlebrush's

sacrificial flowers each day more fervent than the last.
Why should he care if we stared? Who was the ghost?

We emerged out of our own murkiness, shouldering the old
carcasses of words, then disappeared into the distance.

He did not move from the track. This slow time was his
to feast on futures. Later he would make it real.

Why Is a Raven Like
a Writing Desk?

(1)

Obsession is a cover, a screen.
Mostly it's a cover for the diverse, the uncontrollably multiple.
Think about it. But not too much.

Freud wrote of mutilated telegraph messages,
the actual text becoming manifest only in dreams;
(hard not to connect this with the war Freud had just lived
    through).

Distortion by ellipsis.... or omission.

From 1975, for more than ten years, the Japanese
        photographer Masahisa Fukase
photographed ravens. He saw them through train windows,
through the condensation of his own breath. He held them in
    his lens
as dark shadows, black silhouettes, disconnected feathers and
    claws.
Also, as flocks of indistinguishable shapes
lost objects, driven out into space.

'I myself am a raven', he wrote.
Freud's name for Ernst Lanzer was 'Ratman'.
His brothers and sisters nicknamed him 'carrion crow'.

Was Fukase seeing (into) the aftermath of war (as some
        people say) or recording
his own failure and exile? Was it the stillness of photographs
    that fascinated him
or a subject he strained to capture, that flew away from him
    as he got near?

Patients themselves do not know the wording of their own obsessional ideas.

Freud said obsession had to do with self-reproach and then reproaches himself for having got it wrong.

He thought it was one condition when it was many.

A train of thought that leads nowhere.
A train moving through a landscape lost in mist and darkness.

Pathology mobilising reason. Or vice versa.

Ravens have been called requiem birds: birds of death and battlefields.

This was Masahisa Fukase's most famous series of photographs.

They look black but their feathers have multiple reflections: purple, green and blue.

(2)

After my parents died, I found letters I'd written to them years before, when I was living in California. Their pale blue aerogram paper was carefully preserved in a plastic folder. It was as if I were looking through a window at a younger self, a self they'd carefully wrapped and hidden away. I had written to them about taking bicycle rides in the countryside, about the plants and trees I'd seen and the people I met. I mentioned going to the opera with a friend. As I read, in the silence and space of what wasn't there, the memory of heat and sweat comes back to me, the strange sweetness and intensity of the nights, and the sound of trains through the bedroom window in the early mornings.

In one letter I wrote that there had been a fatal hit and run accident on campus and that I'd come upon the aftermath.

The writing brings almost nothing back; or maybe the merest trace. What memory came into being here? Did I see anything? Does the writing know more than I do? Did I push it away by forgetting?

This is the riddle my parents sometimes spell out to me in dreams, where they seem to be still living, in another country, far away.

Seven Descriptions of What Remains

A Bell's *Three Nuns Tobacco* tin, orange and brown.

> A pair of compasses, three erasers, hard as stones,
> a pencil sharpener advertising *Symington's Soup*.

A Morse code machine with the letters of the alphabet down
one side and the equivalent dots and dashes on the other.

> An RAF log book with instructions to use
> indelible pencil to write about 'accidents, or any
> other points of interest connected with the flight'.
> My father has only entered names.

A wooden box (cigar box?) lined with rubber, that contains
files and gouges and delicate chisels for carving (ivory?).

> Flight charts, printed in green ink.

A limpet shell; a black stone in a Perspex box. Two small
bones, curved and mottled, with rounded ends.

Sanctuary

For terrible minutes I searched for the word, like a country
that's missing; thought of the bird flying into the arms
of the figure my father had sketched in a notebook.

This is what matters, he said, grief-struck, unsteady,
grounding himself by holding his pencil up to the light
to measure the distance. A room is a place a story

might begin or end, where doors can open paths
to dreaming. I hear a man's voice over the radio
proclaiming desperate measures in Calais, in Budapest,

in Sofia, in Zagreb. I cannot imagine it: a train station;
a wire fence; the overflowing latrine; children playing
on a stony road. The cold distance between there and here.

My pen scratches paper. Words hinged with cries fly off,
come home to roost. I cannot not imagine it.

Portrait

We'd been talking about how strange the experience was of sitting for a portrait, the artist's gaze intensely personal and yet impersonal at the same time. I recalled how my father had looked at me when he sculpted a bust of me as a young woman, and the confusing sense I had then of shame and self-importance. Because I was still thinking about the conversation the next day, I took a right turn and walked to the corner of Tavistock Square, where Stephen Tomlin's bust of Virginia Woolf (one of several copies) is sited. Apparently, Virginia Woolf hated the experience of being sculpted: sitting still under someone's gaze, unable to escape; 'pinned' as she said in her diary: 'I felt like a piece of whalebone bent'. What was she thinking? A fish out of water, under scrutiny, monstrously large. Or moulded into a corset, stitched into her female inheritance, having to hold just one shape. Because she walked away before the sculpture was completed, her eyes have been left blank; the surface is rough and unfinished. The text added to the plinth underneath restores her to movement and the spontaneous uprush of her own creativity. 'Then one day walking round Tavistock Square I made up, as I sometimes make up my books, To the Lighthouse; in a great, apparently involuntary, rush.'

Cast, cast-down

I bowed my head to the ground

I cast my line into the stream

A fish, a small fish, a thought caught and then returning to
    the stream causing

such a wash and tumult of ideas that it was
impossible to sit still

The next day, I decided to walk to the National Portrait Gallery, but by the time I'd spent an hour pushing through crowds of people, I couldn't face it and turned back.

Later I walked out of the lift at the hotel, and accidentally crossed in front of someone taking a photograph. And there I must have been, a stranger, one of a cast of strangers passing through, blurring the edge of the frame, captured by chance for a moment, moving into and out of visibility.

Disturbance

The light was that blue glow of a summer night. Too hot.
The windows were open and the noises didn't stop. A
   crescendo
of shouting and then someone hammering on a door, kicking
   it down.
She wanted a spliff someone told me, after the police had
   been
and she'd been taken away. These sultry nights
when the inside spills out onto the street.

Through the dark hours I read from the book of
   abandonment:
What then? What if history touches the skin
like an intimate act and there's nowhere to go that isn't it.
Is it the same anger that clothes us that undoes us too?
In the morning carrion crows are flying in circles overhead.
There's a slight breeze, the drawing of breath, the ghost of
   rain.
We sit at the kitchen table, our hands almost touching.

Trinidad

One comes not into the world but into question.
Emmanuel Levinas

1. Bicycle

A blue bicycle sprawls near the road
winding between the Atlantic and the Caribbean.
There are butterflies wavering in the helter-skelter
vegetation of the verge. It's hot, beautiful.
A wooden shack with a rust-scabbed roof
is boarded up – just imagine the prospect
of ocean from those obliterated windows!

We dare not enter, even ourselves,
without having to answer with names and dates,
and history revealing its semantic secrets.
A man in wellingtons is carrying a bucket down
to the beach. He has not seen us; we have not
seen his face. The tide has nowhere to go.
Vultures in wistful regiment are lining the edge.

2. Charles Kingsley in Trinidad, December 1869

My Dear _____

I want to describe everything to you so you can see it
just as I do: the palm tree with leafstalks ten feet long
outside my window; a groo-groo tree split in half –
genus ACROCOMIA – a blaze of yellow flowers
crowning untidy bushes. An orange butterfly flutters
round them, larger than any English kind I've seen.
Behind the cottage is a weedy dell. I call it that
but is that what it is? The slopes surrounding it
are steep as roofs and covered in tufted guinea-grass –
a species spread from Africa, now everywhere.
Some prisoners – soft-eyed – are cutting it for horse feed.
It's hard to know what's garden here, what's forest.

An island paradise we visited had shallows turned to swamp
for lack of tides. In England the sea would quickly drain it.
The stagnant pond was filled with rotting matter
brown and stewed to poison in the sun. The mangroves
do their best to feed on slush and so transform it.
An evil place – a white man would soon die there. I liked
the high woods better. I entered them

                              and fell into a dream:
the colossal shapes of trees towering over me,
a wilderness of creepers, shrubs, utterly impassable,
enormous rounded leaves. Primeval forest as wonderful
as all the travellers have said. And yet

                                     each time I try
to write I come up against my own confusion, helplessness.
Not just the difficulty of finding words. But I can vouch
for nothing here, beyond my senses and what I'm told.
Is God creating versions of new beauty? A story comes to mind:
how Jack found new worlds, a castle and a giant, by climbing
a magic beanstalk. I'm peering up into a cloud of green.

For forty years I've wanted to come here. How can I return?
Will I, Gulliver-like, see our noble trees like broomsticks
planted in the ground, sink into gloom and darkness? I've
    tried
to fill in blank places on the map for others, writing it all
    down.
But what if I, cutlass in hand, am scything everything away,
all I've known
                    not knowing it.

3. Hummingbirds

The Silk-cotton tree stands by a twisting road
high up in the Amerindian mountains.

We parked the car nearby, sheltering
in its shade, before climbing up further.

The tree was never our destination
though it was part of the story he told us

citing, as he did so, Charles Kingsley who
also wrote about how this tree

(Kapok, to us) was haunted by spirits,
and thus (blessedly) escaped decimation.

All the time the hummingbirds flickered around us

Though he wanted us to draw the conclusion
that this was how stories worked, serving

a purpose never the story itself,
he also was part of our story, resisting

the interruptions of someone, a tourist,
bored by his long-windedness. So it went on,

backward and forward, with neither able
to arrest the flow or say all they meant.

Oh lightness laden with shadow. Inseparable wingbeats

Fire

It was because I dreamt it twice it stayed with me:
first the lion roaring at the fire, inside it, yet surviving;

then me, in some lonely place, with fire blazing across a
    hillside
and a forest cutting off the ways I could escape.

My father dreamt of fire before he died. I remember
him waking up, not quite in the world, speaking of how he
    could

plunge into the flames of his own vision. Fire blinds us;
we can't see what feeds the blaze from underneath:

this is Lacan. He was writing about another dream
and another father, roused by his child's voice and a warning

of a death already past. Always it's hard to know
what's real. One script contains allusions to another;

reverberations, voices, carry between dreams;
sense flickers across what divides us from completion.

Intermezzo

(1)

This is a time of transition:
the light is settling for less and less
of forest and wilderness.
Our edges dissolve.
We put on our moth faces.

Some creature flutters through
the veils of darkness,
leaving its perch of centuries.
Before our eyes, it is busy
hemming us into the invisible.

(2)

Will the paths ever meet? On what ground?
Holm-oaks and hawthorns are visors,

green lattice-work, but only partly.
Seeing within seeing, your mind's eye.

The berries bleed into each other.
You come nearer as you write, never

arriving: gap, hesitation, hiatus.
A ruined farmhouse is sinking into

a dark memory riddled with light.
The body cries out without metaphor.

Echoes cross misalignments of time.
No harmony comes yet to assuage you.

As though nurses dashed down a ward to save
a life, and all you can do is wait.

(3)

The notebook you left out overnight is
cold to the touch. You leaf through its pages.

Uncertain compass. Interrupted passageways.
You cast away from safety only
to trail off in silence. Broken lines assail

and beckon.

                    Arrival is a myth.
Here on the page are the spaces your hand
hovered over
                    unwritten penumbra,
spirit presences revealed in the light
afterwards
                    taking life from hiddenness.

Paper-thin store you must return to:
the proximate unknown, belated quickening.

Hide

We perch behind a chink in unseeing
like awkward guests, not yet welcome,

defer, unsure of the distance we are
facing. This is not a place to settle.

We fall into stillness as if treading water.
Emptiness is never single:

there's vanishing, what we were bequeathed
in the anteroom, the station before

the one we alight at. The world is already
happening. In time, we see how the sky

is flourishing, the almost colour against which
an alphabet of lapwings is scattered,

rearranging the words of a letter that arrives
in that other place we read with our hearts first.

1953

The year of the great storm. In Aberdeen enormous waves washed over the sea walls and breached the defences.

People were bent double, stick figures against a huge sky, blown forward or backward by the force of the wind or struggling to move at all. Masonry and tiles spun past them as if everything had become airborne, had acquired the lightness of dry leaves or paper.

It was the year my grandmother died.

From the attic window I could stand on tiptoe and just see the sea, the grey horizon, bitter winds rattling the windowpanes.

Or I stood beside the stiff green brocade curtains in the living room, my camel coat already buttoned up, waiting for something I didn't know, staring down the hill to where my grandmother lived. The weight of the granite church was to my right. The angle of the street and the doors and archways also seemed to be the features of a forbidding look.

Maybe she was already dead.

She had once given me a yellow box with glass bottles that still smelled of lavender and a silver powder compact that had a lever that you pushed forward to scrape out the white powder. I came upon these objects from time to time, as if I had lost them and found them again though, probably, they had been in the same place all the time and I had simply forgotten.

Later my mother told me how my grandmother had died. She described how the saucepans had been neatly stacked to the right of the gas oven.

Somewhere I already knew. But whether the memory was too far away or too close, the distances mixed up with each other, I couldn't make up my mind.

Church

(1)

The church was our shadow
cold November nights, crossing
the road after school,

the lime trees lined up
behind the railings
like staring policemen.

In his black uniform
my grandfather floats
into the house

white hands fluttering
without benediction on Sundays,
trying to find warmth

lurking behind the radio or TV,
that have become cold and silent, suffering
the affront of sin.

(2)

I was four when he lived with us,
when he looked out at the trees
and praised their most lovely foliage.

Six months on and he knew he was
getting over the shock of it:
the smell of gas, her

strange blue skin.
Mrs Stephen brings him fish
every Friday and Miss Walker

bakes a cake and gives him eggs.
He counts his blessings:
his family, his old parishioners.

'We are in God's hands', he writes;
also, 'from now on I must
climb the pulpit steps carefully'.

Shoes

Derrida talked about the patience of shoes,
as he argued with an imaginary other. This could be
how poems go. Uncoupled, detached,
they cannot take a step without you. Devoted
like Greyfriar's Bobby at the grave of his master,
waiting, convinced of an extraordinary resurrection

that does not come. Or maybe it happens elsewhere
and you don't know how you got there –
where your father is sitting in the kitchen near
the high window with the polish and the brushes
and the buffers taking his time with this ordinary task –
dead for how many years? – making the shoes shine.

Walking the Line

The mountain turned into a square
as we descended, then the rain began;
the waiter had a moustache that hung down
like a wet rag. Johnny Cash was crooning
from a jukebox: *Because you're mine,*
I walk the line. Two guitars were propped
in the corner. Our map was coming apart.
We were between places. I stared
into the valley at dark reserves
of woodland, folds of olive groves disappearing
into the hillside. Where were we heading?
Towards what? These questions were
also a matter of time. In a film
we became smaller and smaller in the distance.
History was pressing down,
pressing on. Only in a widening caesura
would the secret outpace the words.
I listened to the break in Cash's voice
and knew he'd got it wrong; we were all
lost and the lines had a way of going straight
to the precipice, never the heart.

Lineage

And then there was Horace-Bénédict de Saussure
who climbed Mont Blanc in 1787.

The magnificent mountains. Mist all around.
He could be in the middle of a stormy sea.

Memory was deceptive like footholds
on a granite crag. Once he saw a couple topple

over a precipice, hand in hand, on their
wedding day. Instruction to self:

Write everything down. His final list comprised
three-hundred and twenty-seven questions.

For instance: *what is the size and nature
of the land of which mountains are composed?*

*Have the strata been deposited by stagnant water
or transported by violent movement?*

Also: *to prevent slipping I recommend iron-cramps.*
Broken cliffs and misty days.

Glaciers cradled between dark forests;
the viscous movement he thought he understood.

*There is no traveller who has nothing to observe.
Keep tools at hand to make repairs.*

*

*Always write in the moment. There is a truth
that cannot afterwards be transcribed.*

And even now his great-grandson Ferdinand
is slipping, unknown, between the lines.

Ferrobo

Stones, shards, rubble, flakes of tile and plaster
are scattered
               unhinged
                              ground into ground.

Wildflowers glisten: cistus and lavender
a chorus
               swaying across hillsides.

One site folded in another.
                    Beneath
a pale blue sky, goats reach into branches
to tear them, pull them down
                       then vanish.
An owl flies across a field before dark.

Surfaces equivocate, encased
in memory
               mosaic of fading

symbols. Weathered histories are

stripped and conjoined out of hearing.

I'm hovering here, a poet once wrote,
over the fragments the ruins.

Eugene Schieffelin and the Starlings

He lets them go with a Shakespearean gesture,
as a curtain of snow falls in Central Park.

Ill-fated sparrows, reluctant passerines,
wilting larks. All these in time

become dull-feathered corpses. He does not stop.
Dark wings gather on the frosty rooftops.

They are readying themselves to vault
ambitiously. Each squawk

imitates an actor imitating a king.
They fly away on the breath of his imagining.

How one man's ego can beget a tragedy!
We're behind a window like Tippi Hedren

as words multiply, hurtle at us,
a murmuration of consequences.

Photograph

A photograph is more than one memory. Time collides
across a particular space; a murky river spills
on to the shore. Remember how you were travelling
in another country. Boats passed you; people living on boats.
You see objects: flowers propped in a bucket by the logs;
clothes pegged to the line; oil drums tied
for ballast to the sides of a perilous raft. Poems are
not always finished. There's a face in the shadow
you can't explain, never saw before, have no story for.
You held the lens steady to tell the future what
you cannot know. The aperture of an instant. In a dream
your mother comes back as she has before, not dead,
but far away, travelling. The lack of connection
disturbs you. You are sorry you have forgotten.

Fence

I've lived with his fence for a decade now. Six foot overlap
panels from Wickes in Autumn Gold, sprayed with Cuprinol

to make doubly sure. I've not seen the garden beyond
for years. Not seen the leaves change colour, in spite

of the red berries, their hectic warning. I felt sorry for him at
first.
He could barely say 'hello', scurried away when I spoke,

always on his own. He piled rubbish in his garden. Burnt it,
a smokescreen, I thought. Then came the first

of the registered letters, phrased carefully, with BSc,
brackets, *Open*, after his name. I saw a window close.

The second letter I refused to collect from the post office.
He added padlocks to the fence, built a fourth shed.

Now he's moving. The fence is down. The field is full of
lapwings.
What kind of damage needs a fence, a wall, razor wire, to
repair it?

Prehension

It's as if in that moment the pencil seized her
red ballet shoes dancing across the page

choreography of text and movement.
Blanchot called it sick, the hand

that grasps at shadows and cannot let go,
holding on to words, as if they were real.

It's the other hand that will rescue her,
closing the notebook, cutting the knots

leading her away from madness
out of darkness into another death.

Nijinsky's Diary

He would call the pen he invented God;
then he thought he could be

God, finding a rhyme within
a rhyme within. Himself. Writing

could not trip him up and let him fall.
What if a machine replayed

the loop of our writing
in perfect simulation without end.

We'd want to become the body dancing.
We'd want our words to fail.

Bay

We got to know the long track to the house
with its dangerous camber, gravel
slipping under our wheels and ragged
patches of mist flying skywards.

There was a sign on a tree, 'Beware of erosion'.
We got to know that too. The great boles
of roots stranded on beaches, gasping
for burial, the cliffs gone soft, defeated.

The sea outstared us. Come here
it said into the masks our faces
had become. We began to see how calm it was
beneath the power, the persistence.

The timbered house creaked. In our dreams
nothing could stop the water edging closer and
closer. Every morning when we woke
the smell of split wood flooded our senses.

Travelling with Elizabeth Bishop

One face laughed/and one face cried; the middle one just
looked.

Under the Window: Ouro Prêto

1.

Too hot, too late, we start along the road.
A carved gate opens on a courtyard;
five ducks bed down beside a rusty car.
Yesterday it rained; today, the mountains,
pencilled grey, are veined by rivulets.
In a muddle of shops and houses someone
is breaking stones, baking bread,
spreading gold leaf on the robe of a saint.
A group of girls giggle at a word we cannot catch.
We climb up to the farm through trees and drooping ferns;
they give us water and news of you
but still we cannot find your home.

2.

On the path to the other side of the island,
ants and beetles leave drifts of cayenne-earth.
The bamboo creaks and cracks, as if
out of its dark forest it speaks to us.
A stray dog waits. He knows even the slightest
response will do. What is the syntax for what is
not yet lost? A small breeze
comes from the ocean. Thunderstorms will
drive away the mountains that drift in and out
of the palest blue. Your words have lodged
themselves in my heart. I forget which day
I must leave this country, not my home.

Letter from an Older Poet

After Marianne Moore

Again an envelope of papery insects
to thank you for.

I loved the grasshopper's spiracles,
the translucent wings; a hint of green

on the thorax. I said to you
years ago, words are like objects,

you should collect what you need.
What's wrong with quoting others?

We're talking about abstraction after all.
And yet I want to hear your voice,

catch your intonation across a continent,
see your face. Dear traveller

I am lost just reading about journeys:
Von Humboldt, Lamarck, Darwin,

all so obsessed; coping with danger like ants
whose home has been stepped on.

Should I try to paint?
My paintbrush's plush is consumed

by moth. I'm looking out for anything
I write that has legs.

Imagine their spindles waving to you,
capsized on the page.

Come back.

Dolphins

A sentinel swallow perched on the rooftop beside the chimney
watches for our departure then swoops into the porch
where its nest is.

Dog-roses along the cliff-top path and the loud name-calling
of kittiwakes, their sea journey before them, perilous over
the froth of the sea.

The dead are with us. We feel their blind inklings, a new
    silence
settling at dusk. Dolphins are breaking the dark surface.
There is more to say.

In the Air

Hands are tracing messages
registering air

it will take a lifetime to decipher
their morphology

the body conducting
its own music, private rests

touching and not touching
the tact of doing neither

of erasing in each gesture what
still catches our breath

Haar

You dream you are standing in the lane beside
your childhood home, the hard-packed earth
scuffed but impenetrable, the walls

on either side too high to see over.
You know how the haar rolls in,
insisting on nothing, the shiver inside

when you feel the cold swarming
around you. How is it you seem to see
what you cannot see, this crust of a dream,

the bristle of atmosphere hugging you to it.

Cherries

Somewhere in the world they are still
Growing cherries as they did in my childhood.

My grandfather's orchard. The long ladders peeping
Out of the trees.

And disembodied voices
Calling to each other through the cover of leaves.

Phut go the blanks
At intervals, that wouldn't fool anyone

Let alone this gaggle of sharp-beaked raiders
Lining up for their pickings.

What is nostalgia but places trying to ambush
The selves we've already moved on from,

History's desire for itself.
May Duke, Napoleon, Waterloo

My lips taste defeat
From a stranger's hands.

Monks House

Someone has entered the garden.
I hear the latch of the gate click far away.
The bees are buzzing in the hyacinths.

Leonard is talking to Percy under the apple trees,
his voice has a crunch to it, not sour not sweet.
I'm half in a dream

tunnelling through shades of green
to where mother is sitting on the steps by the anemones
looking tired and Victorian.

Nothing is only one thing. I surge and delay. Stop and then
take up my pen. The downs soar like birds' wings. Cherry
    trees
are like breaking waves outside.

Adagio

Where the lapwings had been was
empty and the valley sunk beneath

the light shifting of sun. You clung on
inside the notes as they swayed

between horn and oboe.
This avulsion was the body's argument.

You were somewhere between a field
and a memory. The score was still playing

as you ventured towards where the words
would fuse into you: integument, heart.

Garden

Think of it as a notebook. The raggedness
and blossoming together. A way of entering,
belated, scattered, wind-blown.
Your hands are lined with earth before you know it.
You scoop up handfuls, rest your eye
on a particular nowhere. The same bloom has
multiple silences. Seasons do not matter
not now you are inside a parenthesis,
drilling down under layers of weather.
Who knows, it could happen again like this
or not quite like this. You will drive
over the brow of the hill. You will hear
the curlew's song and it will wake something.
It will be a sort of beginning.

Kingfisher

That summer day she turned and called to you
from the river-bank: *hurry – come and see*;

like waking from a dream, struggling
to move or enter another world:

a door flung open, a sudden change
of tense; a gust of wind sweeping through

the orchard at Echoisy, ruffling
the dry grass; the husk of a stranger

left behind on the path as you hurry
forward, and are hurrying still towards

the way you remember it, that crease
in time, the colour it might become

'For Example, My Hand'

Whatever you might think
bodies could be touching on this page

some intimacy left over
or the page itself touching

your hands, for example, holding
the book, and my hand

encoded, transposed, framed
and then maybe not –

crossing circuits, you reading me,
a dusting of pollen on our finger tips.

Notes

The Photographer and The Balloon. The photographer
here is Félix Nadar and the poem draws on an incident in
his memoir, *When I Was a Photographer*, trans. Eduardo
Cadava and Liana Theodratou (MIT Press, 2015), originally
published in French in 1900.

Why Is a Raven Like a Writing Desk? This is the Mad
Hatter's question in Lewis Carroll's *Alice in Wonderland*.
I quote from Freud's 'Some General Characteristics of
Obsessional Structures' and refer to his case study 'Ratman'
(The Standard Edition: Hogarth, 1909), vol. X.

Charles Kingsley In Trinidad. This poem draws on Charles
Kingsley's memoir, *At Last: A Christmas in the West Indies*
(London: Macmillan, 1871).

Fire. 'The Dream of the Burning Child' is one of the dreams
discussed in Freud's *The Interpretation of Dreams* (The
Standard Edition: Hogarth, 1900), vol. V, pp. 339–627.
Freud's interpretation is then discussed by Lacan in
The Four Fundamental Concepts of Psychoanalysis (London:
Penguin), p. 58.

Lineage. Refers to Horace Bénédict de Saussure's *Voyage
dans les Alpes*, 1779–86. A famous geologist in his time, he
was also the great grandfather of the more famous linguist
Ferdinand de Saussure.

Ferrobo. The poet here is C.K. Williams in *Wait*.

Eugene Schieffelin and the Starlings. Eugene Schieffelin
was reputedly responsible for introducing starlings to North
America. He released 60 in Central Park, New York, in 1890;
there are now 200 million spread across the whole of North

America. He did the same with many other birds, mostly unsuccessfully, wanting to introduce to USA all the birds mentioned in Shakespeare.

Prehension. See Maurice Blanchot, *The Space of Literature*, trans. Ann Smock (Lincoln: University of Nebraska Press, 1982).

Nijinsky's Diary. The poem refers to the diary of over 300 pages that the famous ballet dancer wrote in six weeks in 1919 that describes, as it is happening, one of the psychotic episodes which were to plague him for the rest of his life.

Letter from an Older Poet. This poem draws on one of the last published letters Marianne Moore wrote to Elizabeth Bishop in 1969.

In the Air. This poem began as a response to Kate Sweeney's filmed animations of poets' hands.

Monks House. Echoes and phrases from Virginia Woolf's writings drift in here.

'For Example, My Hand'. See Jacques Derrida, *On Touching – Jean-Luc Nancy*, trans. Christine Irizarry (Stanford: Stanford University Press, 2005).

Acknowledgments

Thanks are due to the editors of the following publications where these poems, or versions of these poems, first appeared:

Poetry Review, PN Review, The Rialto, Blackbox Manifold.

'Cherries' was published in the *Arvon Poetry Competition Anthology*, 2010.

Some of these poems were first published in a pamphlet, *Greenhouse*, by Mariscat Press 2013.

'In the Air' was first published in *Poetics of the Archive*, Newcastle Poetry Festival, 2015.

'Crossing' was first published in a pamphlet, *Waves and Bones*, Newcastle Centre for the Literary Arts, Newcastle University, 2018.

I wish to thank all these people who have read and commented on some of these poems: Neil Astley, John Challis, Christy Ducker, Linda France, Cynthia Fuller, Pippa Little, Lisa Matthews, Theresa Muñoz, Sean O'Brien, Ellen Phethean, Anne Ryland, Kate Sweeney, Anna Woodford.

Deryn Rees-Jones has been a patient and insightful editor and I am grateful to her for her careful reading and judicious edits.

My gratitude as always to Ann Spencer, my first reader.